Silly Races

Written by Roderick Hunt
Illustrated by Alex Brychta

OXFORD

UNIVERSITY PRESS

Kipper ran.

Kipper got a banana.

Mum ran.

She got an apple.

Biff and Chip ran.

They got an orange.

Dad ran.

Floppy ran.

Oh no! Dad fell.

Dad got a duck!

Talk about the story

Why are they silly races?

Which race do you think is the funniest?

Which of the races would you like to be in?

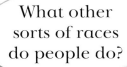

What other sorts of races do people do?

Spot the difference

Find the five differences in the two paddling pools.